Best Friends

Fiona Waters is one of the most prolific and very best anthologists in the children's book world. Her work includes *Glitter When You Jump*, *The Poetry Book*, *Love*, *Why does my mum always iron a crease in my jeans?* and *Don't Panic: 100 Poems to Save Your Life*. Her unparalleled knowledge of poetry and children's books has come about, in part, through Fiona's previous incarnations as a bookseller, publisher, reviewer, author and current position as Editorial Director of Troubadour, the highly successful school book-fair company.

Fiona lives in Dorset surrounded by thousands of books and some very discerning cats.

Michael Broad lives in London. He studied illustration at Portsmouth University, where he first discovered a passion for books. Michael now works solely on writing and illustrating books for children of all ages.

Other books available from Macmillan Children's Books

Wizard Poems
Chosen by Fiona Waters

Fairy Poems
By Clare Bevan

More Fairy Poems
By Clare Bevan

Read Me and Laugh
A Funny Poem for Every Day of the Year
Chosen by Gaby Morgan

Look Out! the Teachers are Coming
Poems chosen by Tony Bradman

Best Friends

Poems chosen by Fiona Waters

Illustrated by Michael Broad

MACMILLAN CHILDREN'S BOOKS

First published 2006 by Macmillan Children's Books
a division of Macmillan Publishers Limited
20 New Wharf Road, London N1 9RR
Basingstoke and Oxford
www.panmacmillan.com

Associated companies throughout the world

ISBN-13: 978-0-330-43789-9
ISBN-10: 0-330-43789-5

3 5 7 9 8 6 4 2

A CIP catalogue record for this book is available from
the British Library.

Printed and bound in Great Britain by Mackays of Chatham plc, Kent

Contents

People Need People Benjamin Zephaniah   1

People Charlotte Zolotow   4

Best Friends Steve Turner   6

For Now Sue Cowling   7

What Is a Best Friend For? Matt Simpson   8

A Huggle John Lyons   10

Dragon Love Poem Roger Stevens   11

My Friend Dee Dave Ward   12

The Perfect Friend Clare Bevan   13

Recipe for a Birthday Angela Topping   14

My Friend Mountain Flower Benjamin Zephaniah   16

That's You and Me! Ian Souter   18

Mirror Friends Jamila Gavin   20

Sarah Gillian Floyd   22

my friend Emily Hearn   24

two friends Nikki Giovanni 26

What I'd Do for My Best Friend Gerard Benson 28

Laura Jeff Moss 30

Last Lick Valerie Bloom 32

Starting School Geraldine Aldridge 34

Where Is Everybody? Dave Calder 37

My Best Friend: the Astronaut Ian Larmont 39

You Are What's in Your Pockets Lindsay MacRae 40

All Friends Should Be Like This Caroline Rose 43

Mobile Marnie Francis de Carle 45

Me, Myself, I Chrissie Gittins 47

Calling Names Irene Rawnsley 48

One-to-One Lynne Taylor 49

The Best Dad Steve Turner 50

Love Me Mum Brenda Williams 51

My Best Friend Angela Topping 52

She's My New 'Best Friend' Trevor Harvey 54

Man's Best Friend Mike Jubb 55

Dogs Frances Cornford 56

Cat Warmth John Cunliffe 57

The Hairy Dog Herbert Asquith 58

Cat-Value Grace Nichols 59

Simple Addition Pat Gadsby 60

Miss Antrobus Richard Edwards 61

Best of Friends Clare Bevan 62

The Awfullest of Friends Brian Patten 64

Pass it on Lemn Sissay 66

A Falling Out Matt Simpson 67

Skipping Rope Sue Cowling 68

Three Chrissie Gittins 70

Balancing Pat Gadsby 71

I'm Sorry Roger Stevens 72

I'm Sorry I'm Sorry I'm Sorry Lemn Sissay 73

Tich Miller Wendy Cope 74

Crushed Sandy Brownjohn — 76

New Boy Gareth Owen — 78

Stay in Touch Lindsay MacRae — 80

Snollygoster Helen Dunmore — 82

And I Went Roger Stevens — 84

Sonnet Number One Roger Stevens — 86

Breaking Up – and Making Up Trevor Harvey — 87

Patagonian Friendship Poem Jennifer Curry — 88

People Need People

To walk to
To talk to
To cry and rely on,
People will always need people.
To love and to miss
To hug and to kiss,
It's useful to have other people.
To whom will you moan
If you're all alone,
It's so hard to share
When no one is there,
There's not much to do
When there's no one but you,
People will always need people.

To please
To tease
To put you at ease,
People will always need people.
To make life appealing
And give life some meaning,
It's useful to have other people.
If you need change
To whom will you turn,
If you need a lesson
From whom will you learn,
If you need to play
You'll know why I say
People will always need people.

As girlfriends
As boyfriends,
From Bombay
To Ostend,
People will always need people.
To have friendly fights with
And share tasty bites with,
It's useful to have other people.
People live in families,
Gangs, posses and packs,
It seems we need company
Before we relax,
So stop making enemies
And let's face the facts,
People will always need people,
Yes
People will always need people.

Benjamin Zephaniah

People

Some people talk and talk
and never say a thing.
Some people look at you
and birds begin to sing.

Some people laugh and laugh
and yet you want to cry.
Some people touch your hand
and music fills the sky.

Charlotte Zolotow

Best Friends

Best friends tell you secrets
Best friends always play
Best friends send you postcards
When they go away.

Best friends guess your thinking
Best friends read your eyes
Best friends notice right away
If you're telling lies.

Best friends say they're sorry
Best friends say they care
Best friends may be absent
But they're always there.

Steve Turner

For Now

If I can change the world for you
one day,
won't that be grand!

For now I'll fetch the tissues,
mop your tears
and hold your hand.

Sue Cowling

What Is a Best Friend For?

Being with,
Telling jokes to,
Walking home with,
Telling worries to,
Listening to CDs with,
Sitting next to,
Playing games with,
Trusting secrets to,
Doing homework with,
Showing your poems to,
Someone you miss when they're not there,
Someone you know will really care
As much as you when *you're* not there.

Matt Simpson

A Huggle

A huggle
is more than a snuggle.
It's different from a cuddle.

A snuggle has got to be right,
a cuddle is sometimes tight,
squeezing away softness;

but a huggle
is soft and warm,
full of arms.

It's even better
than treacle toffee.

John Lyons

Dragon Love Poem

When you smile
The room lights up

and I have to call
the fire brigade

Roger Stevens

My Friend Dee

My friend Dee
Is bigger than me,
And I'm more than three feet tall.

My friend Dee
Is bigger than me –
She can see over next-door's wall.

Whenever she looks over,
She laughs and giggles
Or runs and hides
And screams and shivers,
But she *never* tells me
What it is she can see . . .
Of course *I'm* not bothered at all.

Dave Ward

The Perfect Friend

I have a simply PERFECT friend
Who saves my place at table,
Who asks me to her birthday treats
Whenever she is able.

She takes me on her outings
To the seaside or the zoo,
She tells me all her troubles
And her hopes – as best friends do.

We never fight or stamp our feet,
We love each other dearly –
And though I am INVISIBLE,
My friend can see me clearly.

Clare Bevan

Recipe for a Birthday

Ingredients:

One clear morning
Birthday paper
Presents bought in secret
Icing sugar
The right number of little candles
A cake to stick them in
People to sing
Friends' faces
All smiles

Method:

Mix together
Simmer all day
Tuck up in bed when done.

Angela Topping

My Friend Mountain Flower

She dresses in a thousand beads
   Each year she plants a thousand seeds.

With skill she weaves her wicker baskets
   She weaves her people's sleeping blankets.

She may not have what we call wealth
   But she can build her house herself.

Although she still lives with her mom
   Experts can't work out where she's from.

She comes from a village people
  They're famous for being peaceful.

If she gets married she won't roam
  Her husband must live in her home.

Some say that with the passing years
  Her way of life just disappears.

She's my friend, and you can quote me,
  Mountain Flower is a Hopi.

Benjamin Zephaniah

That's You and Me!

As friends we:

whisper,
discuss,
argue
then float messages across a crowded playground
that only we know and understand.

As friends we:

walk,
stumble,
run
then spring after each other
so close we exchange shadows as we go.

As friends we:

laugh,
cry,
care
then taste each other's thoughts
and share each other's moods.

One girl, one boy,
one friendship to enjoy.
One lock, one key,
that's you and me!

Ian Souter

Mirror Friends

When we look in the mirror,
Me and my friend,
I am brown and she is white.
When we look in the mirror,
Me and my friend,
My hair is dark and hers is light.

And my eyes are black as a raven's wing,
And hers are as blue as a sapphire ring.
She likes chips
And I like rice,
She likes ketchup
And I like spice.

But when we look in the mirror,
Me and my friend,
We feel we are the same as same can be,
Though I am brown and she is white,
We could be sisters,
She and me.

Jamila Gavin

Sarah

Sarah's my best friend.
She's the one I tell my secrets to
And she tells me hers;
And if we have troubles and cares
We tell each other those as well:
No one else knows.

It's great to have a friend
Like Sarah.
We go everywhere, do everything
Together –
Like eat our lunch, do our homework,
Comb each other's hair.
People say that we're joined at the hip,
Or that we're just like twins:
I think they're right.

Sometimes I wonder
What I would be like without my friend.
I think I'd be
A little wooden fishing-boat
Tossed by an angry sea,
A single tiny star
Twinkling in an endless night,
A butterfly blown by the wind.
It makes me sad
To think that could be me;

But then I think of my best friend
And I feel glad –
Glad that she's my friend,
That Sarah's my best friend.

Gillian Floyd

my friend

my friend is
like bark
rounding a tree

he warms
like sun
on a winter day

he cools
like water
in the hot noon

his voice
is ready
as a spring bird

he is
my friend
and I
am his

Emily Hearn

two friends

lydia and shirley have
two pierced ears and
two bare ones
five pigtails
two pairs of sneakers
two berets
two smiles
one necklace
one bracelet
lots of stripes and
one good friendship

Nikki Giovanni

What I'd Do for My Best Friend

I have a friend. Her name is Fleur,
And I'd do anything for her.

If my friend Fleur was kept in late,
I'd wait for her by the snicket gate.

If my friend Fleur slipped down a drain,
I'd try and pull her out again.

If she was down a deep dark hole,
I'd fish her out with a great long pole.

If my friend Fleur was put in jail,
I'd pay a million pounds in bail.

If she fell off our garden wall,
I'd compliment her on her fall.

But if she was really scared at night,
I'd let her borrow my night light.

If my friend Fleur was up the creek,
I'd go and see her every week.

If my best friend was in a stew,
I wouldn't eat it. Well, would you?

If Fleur was eaten by a lion,
I don't think I would ever stop cryin'.

If she was eaten by a gerbil,
I wouldn't laugh. (Though I might burble.)

Cos she's my friend, my very best friend.
That's all I've got to say.

The End

Gerard Benson

Laura

Laura's new this year in school.
She acts so opposite, it seems like a rule.
If someone says yes, Laura says no.
If someone says high, Laura says low.
If you say bottom, she'll say top.
If you say go, she'll say stop.
If you say short, Laura says tall.
If you say none, she says all.
If you say beginning, Laura says end . . .
but today she asked me to be her friend.
I said maybe
but not quite yes.
Then I said, 'Want to take a walk?'
And Laura said, 'I guess.'

Jeff Moss

Last Lick

Sue and me walk home from school together every
   day,
We play 'teacher' and 'hide an' seek' and 'tag' along
   the way,
But the best game is the one we always leave until
   the end,
Till just before we reach her gate, right beside the
   double bend.
Sue always get me first, but she won't get me today.
So as she reaching out her hand, I jump out of the
   way,
Then before she know, I stretch out my hand and
   touch her quick,
And as I racing down the road, I holler out, 'LAST
   LICK!'

Valerie Bloom

Starting School

New school today. Big heavy door.
I've never been in here before.
New clothes and shoes that hurt my feet,
new teachers, boys and girls to meet.
Older children round the school
make me feel so very small.
Here's my classroom. Find a space.
Teacher with a smiling face.
Lots of children I don't know
all quickly find the way to go.

Playtime now. We all go out.
Bigger children run about.
I'll go and stand beside that tree.
A little girl comes up to me.
She says, 'Can I stand next to you?
I'm new. Do you know what to do?'
We find we live quite near each other,
my brother Kenny knows her brother.
She says can she be friends with me.
She's coming round today for tea.

Geraldine Aldridge

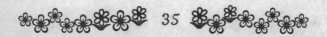

Where Is Everybody?

Here we are, two weeks into the summer holidays,
and there's no one around. It's not
like Alasdair who went to Loch Ard
or Cafy who went to Iran
and never came back. It's not
even like Ola who went to Bearsden
or Emma who changed schools
and was hardly seen again.
It's not even like Cassy whose mum's
full of twins and moving house.
I can understand them. It's life.
People move. But this is strange – there's
no one. I go to the supermarket, to the park,
and there's no one I even know. I ring their bells,
I ring them up – no one answers. They can't
all be away. It's as if they'd all gone
on holiday together, to a party without inviting me.
I play with this and that, I watch telly, read comics,
sometimes go swimming or get taken places.

I even play with toddlers. I go to the gardens,
kick a ball, hide in trees.
But there's a big hole inside me. I keep
expecting my friends to jump from the bushes
shouting surprise. I wonder
who'll be there when school starts again.
Will I be in a class of one?

Dave Calder

My Best Friend: the Astronaut

My best friend is an astronaut,
And she wrestles bears for fun,
And *she* never has to have a bath,
And she carries a proton gun.

She never wears her wellies
In the wet, to go to school.
She's cheeky to my teacher
And she has broken every rule.

She never eats her cabbage,
And gets texts from China too.
Next week, she starts a brand-new job,
With tigers, in the zoo.

She is *great*! My friend the astronaut,
Her rocket is gold and red.
She's flying it, with me, right now,
Around and round my bed.

Ian Larmont

You Are What's in Your Pockets

What are little boys made of?

One blunt pencil, badly chewed;
A battery you always lose
But which then turns up again;
Grit, fluff, someone else's pen.
Matter that once filled your nose
Or lived in between your toes –
Whatever it is,
It's green and glows:
That's what boys are made of.

What are little girls made of?

Scrunched-up tissues, old hair-clips,
Some foul-tasting gloop for lips;
Notes which say: 'YOU'RE NOT MY FRIEND!';
Grit, fluff, someone else's pen.
Sticky, purple glittery stuff
Of which you can never have enough;
Chocolate –
For when the going gets tough:
That's what girls are made of.

Lindsay MacRae

All Friends Should Be Like This

An anxious-listener
A friendly-cover
An animal-lover
A brainy-writer
A sweet-liker
A mystery-adventurer
A low-whisperer
An always-forgiver
A good-truster
A comforting-soother
A pleasant-talker
A polite-eater
An understanding-partner
An interesting-storyteller.

Caroline Rose

Mobile

Te de dum . . . te de dum . . . te de dum dum
  Ah, that's my best friend,
    not shouting
    or waving –
    just serenading!
  And if I don't want to talk
    it's all in store,
    perhaps heaps more.
  I'll catch up when I go for a walk.

Te de dum . . . te de dum . . . te de dum dum
  Sorry, that's for me.
    it's just not cool
    to call at school,
  mobiles in class against the rule
    but it's great to know you care.
    Without my phone
    I'm home alone.
  Now someone's always there.

Marnie Francis de Carle

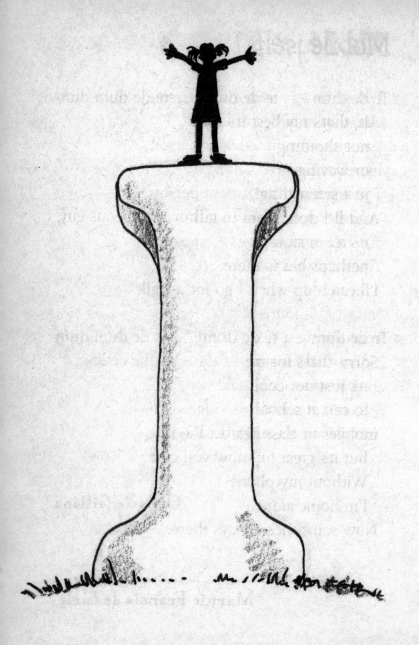

Me, Myself, I

You are a very important person,
You always have a CAPITAL 'I',
You are a very important person,
I speak no word of a lie,
You are a very important person,
Whether you're a cool girl or a gorgeous guy,
You're a very important person,
You deserve a CAPITAL 'I'.

In fact, without a doubt,
You deserve a CAPITAL 'I'
Which climbs straight through the ceiling
And hits the clear blue sky
Where a dragonfly is singing,
'Can I have a CAPITAL "I"?'

Chrissie Gittins

Calling Names

I call my brother
Waggle Ears, Banana Boots
And Nobble Nose.

He calls me Mop Head,
Turnip Top,
Potato Pie and Twinkle Toes.

I call him Weed,
He calls me Wimp
Then Mum comes in the door.

She calls us Double Trouble
Then we're both
Best friends once more.

Irene Rawnsley

One-to-One

all my friends have
a mum and dad
or mum and stepdad
or dad and stepmum
or mum and her boyfriend
or dad and his girlfriend

I just have a dad
the best friend I've ever had

Lynne Taylor

The Best Dad

My dad's much weaker than your dad
My dad's got less hair on his head
My dad snores louder than your dad
My dad spends more time in bed.

My dad's much weirder than your dad
My dad's got more flakes up his nose
My dad's less trendy than your dad
My dad wears more awful clothes.

My dad's more sober than your dad
My dad's got more wax in his ears
My dad talks dafter than your dad
My dad looks older by years.

My dad's got less teeth than your dad
My dad's got more sweat in his pits
My dad's much plumper than your dad
That's why I love him to bits.

Steve Turner

Love Me Mum

Love me
Even though I sulk for days.
Love me
Even when I answer back.
Love me
Even when I get in trouble.
Love me Mum
For I love you.

I love you
Even when I rant and rave.
I love you
Even when I'm in a mood.
I love you
Even when I'm nagging on.
I love you
For I'm your mum.

Brenda Williams

My Best Friend

We stand on the river-bank
while he shows me
where trout lie.

He knows the names
of all wild things
in the earth and sky.

He taught me colours
and animal prints,
bought me a kite.

We laugh a lot.
He tells old jokes
to make things right.

We play cards for money –
old pennies he's saved.
He's my best mate.

He buys me chips
in a drippy vinegar bag.
My grandad's great.

Angela Topping

She's My New 'Best Friend'

I like my Doctor most of all.

(She's given me a week off school.)

Trevor Harvey

Man's Best Friend

My mum says,
'A friend in need is a friend indeed.'
But,
my dad says,
'A friend on a lead
can get you out of the house.'

Mike Jubb

Dogs

I had a little dog,
   and my dog was very small.
He licked me in the face,
   and he answered to my call.
Of all the treasures that were mine,
   I loved him best of all.

Frances Cornford

Cat Warmth

All afternoon,
My cat sleeps
On the end of my bed.

When I creep my toes
Down between the cold sheets,
I find a patch of cat-warmth
That he's left behind;
An invisible gift.

John Cunliffe

The Hairy Dog

My dog's so furry I've not seen
His face for years and years:
His eyes are buried out of sight,
I only guess his ears.

When people ask me for his breed,
I do not know or care:
He has the beauty of them all
Hidden beneath his hair.

Herbert Asquith

Cat-Value

An alarm clock purring in the morning,
A furry hot-water bottle at night,
A torch-light with two little beams in the dark,
Value for money all right.

Grace Nichols

Simple Addition

4	LARGE PAWS
2	FLOPPY EARS
2	BRIGHT EYES
1	WET NOSE
1	WAGGY TAIL
═	BEST FRIEND

Pat Gadsby

Miss Antrobus

Why do you love your octopus,
Miss Antrobus, Miss Antrobus?
Why do you love your octopus,
Miss Antrobus, my dear?

I love my octopus because
It hugs me and it wriggles,
I love my octopus because
Its wriggles give me giggles,
I love my octopus because
It juggles jars of pickles,
I love my octopus because
It tickles, oh, it tickles!

Richard Edwards

Best of Friends

Me and my friend
Love to fight,
Make it up
Every night.

In the playground
Every day,
Can't agree
Which game to play.

In the classroom
When we're writing,
Elbows, knees
Are always fighting.

In PE and
When we're dressing,
Nudge and niggle
Every lesson.

After school and
Down the street,
Grabbing bags or
Tripping feet.

Quarrel now and
Argue later.
She's my BEST friend,

And I HATE her.

Clare Bevan

The Awfullest
of Friends

Alan shouts at Alice,
Alice snaps at Sue,
Sue scowls at William
(It's like living in a zoo).

Andrew curses Sarah,
Sarah moans at John,
John despises Matthew
And wishes he was gone.

Jerry curses Tony,
Tony snarls at Tess,
Tess says Tina's boring
And that she looks a mess.

Sam finds Pete repulsive,
Pete thinks Josh is vile,
Josh says Gita's childish
And Patrick's infantile.

Edward jeers at Sadie,
Sadie laughs at Paul,
Paul says Zoe's stupid
And he hates them all.

I want to leave this party,
I'm not happy any more,
I used to like these people,
But now I'm not so sure.

Brian Patten

Pass it on

Tell Brian to tell Jane to tell Janine
to tell Germaine to tell June to tell Maxine
to tell Linda to tell Lucinda to tell Mel
to tell Genet to tell Mesrat to tell Del
to tell Ashraf to tell Akin to tell Jimmy
to tell Nadia to tell Nazreen to tell Timmy
to tell Lynn to tell Jim to tell Anne
to tell Jill to tell Joanne to tell Jan
to tell Joe to tell Jack to tell John
that I'm not talking to him or anyone!

Lemn Sissay

A Falling Out

You're not MY FRIEND any more!
Why'd you have to tell
Miranda Wilson all those things?
That Karen Flynn as well?

Things we swore were secret,
Strictly between us two,
Cross-your-heart-and-hope-to-die things
Only the two of us knew.

It's really disgusting me to see
You sucking up to her.
Couldn't you tell how I was feeling
From the way you saw me glare?

Well, it's too late now to say sorry,
To make things all OK,
I just can't trust you any more,
So put your Smarties away!

Matt Simpson

Skipping Rope

She thinks I'll mope
When it's time for play
And she whisks you off
Like yesterday

But her eyes will pop
When she sees me spend
This playtime
With my new best friend

Going   forwards
backwards
skip-skip-skipping
crossing hands
and never tripping

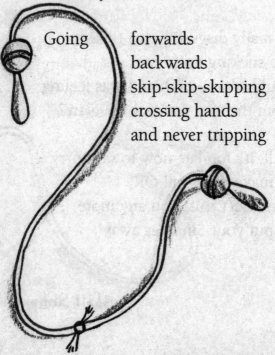

Much too busy
For her to see
If what she's doing
Matters to me

And she'll realize
That bullies don't win
When she sees the others
Joining in

Going   forwards
              backwards
              skip-skip-skipping
              crossing hands
              and never tripping.

Sue Cowling

Three

My best friend *has* a best friend,
she is a bester friend than me,
but when they have a falling out
my friend is best with me.

Chrissie Gittins

Balancing

Being a good friend
Like walking a tightrope
Is a balancing act
Wonderful when it works but
They both hurt when you fall

Pat Gadsby

I'm Sorry

As I lie here in bed
These words chase round my head
I'm sorry

Our head teacher said
That words can't be unsaid
I'm sorry

I called you scraggy bones
I called you maggot pie
I'm sorry

And when you cried, I laughed
I said, I hope you die
I'm sorry

I've been awake for hours
Tomorrow I will try to say
I'm sorry

Roger Stevens

I'm Sorry I'm Sorry I'm Sorry

It was the way you stopped – mid laugh
The moment I said it I knew I shouldn't have
I didn't mean to say it. Not the way that I did
I didn't mean it – the way it sounded
What I mean is I said it but the wrong way round
When I said it I read it again in your frown
It shouldn't have come out, I should have kept it in
Not that it was in if you see what I am saying
I'm sorry I'm sorry I'm sorry. What I mean to say is
  I regret it
I pushed it over the edge, I did. I sensed it when I
  said it

Lemn Sissay

Tich Miller

Tich Miller wore glasses
with elastoplast-pink frames
and had one foot three sizes larger than the other.

When they picked teams for outdoor games
she and I were always the last two
left standing by the wire-mesh fence.

We avoided one another's eyes,
stooping, perhaps, to retie a shoelace,
or affecting interest in the flight

of some fortunate bird, and pretended
not to hear the urgent conference:
'Have Tubby!' 'No, no, have Tich!'

Usually they chose me, the lesser dud,
and she lolloped, unselected,
to the back of the other team.

At eleven we went to different schools.
In time I learned to get my own back,
sneering at hockey players who couldn't spell.

Tich died when she was twelve.

Wendy Cope

Crushed

Out on the edge, where the playground meets the
   grassland,
A little girl is sitting and crying alone.
Over the playground the pigeons are winging
But she doesn't see them, her eyes are stinging
With tears at the insults the others were slinging
To force her to go off and play on her own.

A little girl is sitting and crying her eyes out,
Surrounded by sharp sticks and pointed stones.
High up above her the skylarks are singing
But she doesn't hear them, her ears are still ringing
With all the untruths the others were flinging.
– And these are the words they say cannot break
   bones.

Sandy Brownjohn

New Boy

He stood alone in the playground
Scuffed his shoes and stared at the ground
He'd come halfway through term from the Catholic
  school
On the other side of town.

He'd a brand-new blazer and cap on
Polished shoes and neatly cut hair
Blew on his fists, looked up and half-smiled
Pretending he didn't care.

And I remember when I'd been new
And no one had spoken to me
I'd almost cried as I stood alone
Hiding my misery.

Heart said I should go over
Share a joke or play the fool
But I was scared of looking stupid
In front of the rest of the school.

At break someone said they'd seen him
Crying in the geography test
And when he came out they pointed and laughed
And I laughed along with the rest.

In my dreams I'd always stood alone
Believing I was the best
But in the cold playground of everyday life
I was no better than the rest.

Gareth Owen

Stay in Touch

A lazy teenager called Joan
Never bothered to pick up the phone
    So she missed out on dates
    Lost touch with her mates
And spent every evening alone.

Lindsay MacRae

Snollygoster

Snollygoster
you told me, 'If you give me your KitKat
I won't let Jake Harris kick you,'

Snollygoster
you said, 'Don't leave your custard
or the dinner lady'll get you,'

Snollygoster
you took my new felt-tip pens
then helped me look for them,

Snollygoster
you pushed me under
when no one was looking,
then you said, 'I was only trying
to teach you how to swim,'

Snollygoster
Snollygoster
I didn't tell my mum
I didn't tell anyone,

but, Snollygoster,
I told myself:
You don't need that Snollygoster
you don't need that felt-tip-stealing
push-you-under
eat-that-custard
no-kick-for-a-KitKat
best friend
Snollygoster.

Helen Dunmore

And I Went

And I went
I don't even know
What you're talking about
And she went
You being funny?
And I went
Is anyone laughing?
What's your problem?
And she went
You looking for a fight?
And I went
Is there one here then?
And she went
You looking at me?
And I went
And she went
And I went
And she went
So I went.

Roger Stevens

Sonnet Number One

The moon doth shine as bright as in the day,
I sit upon the see-saw wondering why
She left me. Boys and girls come out to play.
But I'm bereft. I think I'm going to cry.
I gave her chocolate and I praised her skill
At skateboarding and football, not to mention
Wrestling. As we slowly climbed the hill
To fetch some water, did I sense a tension?
She seemed preoccupied. She hardly spoke
And as we turned the handle to the well
I asked her, Jill, please tell me it's a joke.
She said, I've found another bloke. I fell,
I rolled, head over heels into the dark,
Down to the bottom where I broke my heart.

Roger Stevens

Breaking Up –
and Making Up

Yes, YOU can watch my DVDs
And ride my mountain bike;
Yes, you can wear my Arsenal shirt
As often as you like;
Yes, you can use my iPod
And borrow it all day;
Yes, you can choose computer games
That YOU'd prefer to play.

I'm GLAD you've said that you'll agree
Our quarrel's at an end,
For I've really MISSED you while you weren't
My *very* BEST 'best friend' . . . !

Trevor Harvey

Patagonian Friendship Poem

My friend is a white wave
Calm and strong.

My friend's voice is gentle water
Lapping the shore.

My friend's eyes are dark pools
Among the rocks.

My friend's smile is sunshine
Glittering on the sea.

My friend is the ocean . . .
And I am the golden fish
That swims in her deep waters.

Jennifer Curry